A Month
of Sundays

A Month
of Sundays

COURTNEY PEPPERNELL

Andrews McMeel
PUBLISHING®

Acknowledgments

During a particularly difficult time in my life, I had commitments to a number of book deals. This was one of them. It is through the kindness, compassion, and devotion of my team that I was able to finish this project. My publishers at Andrews McMeel, especially Kirsty, Patty, Danys, Diane, and Liz—thank you for your patience and understanding. My agents, Katherine and James; illustrator, Justin; and personal assistant, Karna—thank you for your untiring support, kindness, and compassion; I cherish the journey that we are on together, and I am so grateful to work with you and call you my friends. My family and my support circle, without you, I wouldn't be standing and I wouldn't be writing; you have given me the space and encouragement to continue doing what I love. My dogs, Hero and Dakota, the lights of my life. My chickens, Annie, Poppy, and Lottie, you bring me joy every day. And, finally, to my readers, in the deepest heartache of my life, you reminded me of a very important thing—when we have poetry, we have hope, and with hope, we can come back from anything.

Instagram: @courtneypeppernell
TikTok: @courtneypeppernell
Facebook: @Courtney Peppernell
Email: courtney@pepperbooks.org

www.peppernell.com

If you dare venture beyond the forest with the tallest evergreen trees, if you are bold enough to travel past the creeks and lakes that freeze, you will find a lonely mountain rising against the sky, rugged and mysterious, ancient and wise; the mountain knows more secrets than you or I. But within the mountain, in the deepest cave, among the moondust and fireflies, lives a guardian with sparkling blue eyes and icicles in their hair, with softness in their heart and purpose in the air. They patrol the woodlands at the first signs of frost, looking for little souls who have become alone and lost.

And so, on the longest and darkest night of the year, with snowflakes dancing in the air, as the guardian glided through the forest, singing a solstice song with a beautiful chorus, they stumbled upon a small hedgehog, forgotten and abandoned in the cold. Life had been harsh and cruel and unkind, and the hedgehog needed a hand to hold and a safe place to find.

The hedgehog was you, and this is the story of a very long winter, a month of Sundays dark and unforgiving, making you question your strength and the very purpose of living. There you were, unraveling at the seams, until the guardian appeared, bright and hopeful between the trees.

"I see you," the guardian said. "You don't have to be alone."

"But alone is all I know," you replied. "I have forgotten what it means to be brave."

And the guardian nodded softly.

"Come with me," they said. "Let us go deep inside the cave."

"Into the darkness?" you replied, uncertain and afraid.

"Yes," the guardian said. "There is much to be learned in the dark, and there is healing to take place. You can say all the things you wish to say and undo all the messy parts of you, for you will be safe in this space, and I will still be here the next day. This I promise to be true."

And you wondered if the cave would accept someone so broken and unsure, that perhaps it would spit you back out, declaring that, for your lost soul, there could be no cure. But the guardian's words enveloped you, warm and sure, offering a promise you had never heard before.

"You will have many winters throughout your time; some will be long, and some short, and others somewhere in between, but you must find a newer you and make peace with all the versions you've ever been—for, in life, we will always heal if we give ourselves permission to rest and a chance to feel."

So, deep into the cave you went, and the further in, the more you understood that even the darkness had some things to teach, despite the stars so far away and so out of reach. Within the cave, you learned to sit with this darkness, acknowledging that perhaps it was just an old friend; you realized the beauty in taking time to uncover all of life's turns and bends. You found perseverance and reveled in all your moments of clarity, discovering that your true beauty lay in your grace and humility. You learned to embrace the change, which in turn allowed you to let love in, for greatness truly blossoms when we choose to grow within. You practiced self-compassion, to be a little kinder to your mistakes, for no soul is ever immune to the way life aches. And, perhaps, above all, you understood a secret older than the mountains themselves—that, while time can never be borrowed, there is still such hope for tomorrow.

When the snow started to melt away and the birds returned to sing, the forest began a new cycle, welcoming once more the spring. And so, from the cave, you emerged, wiser than before you went inside, and you felt the sun wash over you; you were now unafraid to hide. And even though winter will return each and every year, and so, too, the ups and downs of life, hold on to your dreams, and embrace your fears. What you must promise yourself is that, despite the darkness, the most beautiful thing we can learn is that, after every long night, the light will undoubtedly always return.

Author's Note

When I wrote this book, my life changed in a way I had never expected. The person I had loved for many years betrayed me in a way that I believe many people have also experienced. I have listened to many people's similar stories of infidelity over the years; I have heard and seen it all—but, simply put, when it's happening to you, the world feels like it is ending. I sat for many days, weeks, and months, wondering how could I—someone who had always spoken of deep love and connection between people—have been taken for such a fool?

In the aftermath, I did have a very long month of Sundays, the deepest, darkest winter I had ever experienced. I blamed myself. I carried an ache far greater than one I thought I would ever experience in this lifetime, and I felt I would never see, hear, or feel joy again. But a funny thing happens when you stay in a darkened cave with all the quiet and you begin to listen to this darkness. It reminds you of things you had long forgotten. Inside that cave, I was reminded of my strength, that the choices of others were not my fault, that I had given everything to this person, and, in return, I had been treated far worse than I ever deserved. The darkness reminded me of my worth and of the light that had been diminished for far too long.

It gave me hope that I would find my way into blue skies once more.

And I did find my way into blue skies again; I rebuilt myself and my life, I chose new dreams, and I learned to open myself to love again and to be hopeful for the future. The experience taught me that, even in the times we are hurt and the actions of selfish people can force us to go inward, if we remain open, we are reminded that there are still good and beautiful people in this world.

I tell you my own story because it has been the stories of my readers that have held my hand through the dark. I have heard your stories of betrayal and pain, but I have also heard your stories of hope and courage. I am not invisible anymore, and I am not taken for granted. And, yes, it was the hardest lesson I have ever learned, that the person I trusted the most had no respect for me and held no empathy—but the growth from such a lesson was important. In learning to accept this, I have also accepted that I am heard and I am seen. To share this with you, my readers, is a powerful thing.

This is not the end of the road for me; I will continue to walk this path of healing for quite some time. But for those who have been on this journey for a long while, as well as those who have perhaps only very recently joined, I say this: I love jellyfish because they light up the dark; they will always be a symbol for finding light in such darkness, and, no matter where I go, wherever these journeys take me, I know that each jellyfish that accompanies me will always keep me going.

I hope you stay on this journey with me—perhaps we might help each other.

Table of Promises

SIT
WITH DARKNESS

There was once a time in my life when darkness enveloped every part of me. All day and all night, the shadows persisted. There was no sun, no moon, no stars. I was alone, broken, and desperate for a way out. Until, eventually, in a moment of stillness, the darkness spoke to me.

It said, "You do not fear me."

"Yes, I do," I had replied. "I have feared you my whole life."

But the darkness shook its head. "You simply do not know me." The darkness took my hand, and together we walked side by side. Instead of seeing, I listened, to every step and every beat of my heart. And darkness said, "We fear the things we do not understand, but understand this: I am here to remind you, despite the joy of the day and comfort in the light, there will always be lessons to learn in the night."

The skies will grow dark,
and the sun will disappear;
the world will feel too big,
and so too your greatest fear.

But something I ought to share
is that, even on your worst day,
the light hasn't gone anywhere;
it exists in all the things you say
and in all the reasons to stay.

A Month of Sundays

Even after all this time,
there is still fear in the healing.
Not because I do not see the light
but rather I wonder sometimes
if the light sees me.

I hear you in the note
of every sad song,
I see you in the line
of every heartache poem,
I feel you on the days
the skies open and the
rain pours down.

We found each other
at our worst
and for months wanted
to make it work.

I know you tried;
I tried too, and
now someone else
is going to have
the better you.

A Month of Sundays

Sometimes I wonder,
was it too much to ask,
just to have someone stand by me,
build a home, have a family—
was it so wrong to want those things?

Perhaps I was foolish;
I was too young to understand
all the red flags.

I just wanted to grow old with someone,
have my hand held, be cherished by
a love who truly saw my value.

I ache in a thousand different places,
my heart breaks every day,
my mind does not stop.

But it's my soul that hurts the most;
it hurts for me, my entire existence,
all the things I have come to be.

I just don't understand how the person
I gave everything to could be so unkind to me.

There are things I have forgotten, like your mother's favorite color and the name of the street you grew up on. I don't remember all the digits of your phone number or how many blue sweaters you own—but I remember the way your hand felt, the way it used to brush the hair from my eyes. I remember your laugh, how it was warm like a new spring day. And I remember how much it hurt the day everything ended. This is the most painful thing about memory: how do I hold on to all the good without living with all the bad?

The stars will always
need darkness to shine,
just like the moon
will always need
the night to glow.

There is purpose
to the dark.

When you have spent so long
comparing yourself with others,
looking in the mirror and
despising what you see—
it becomes who you are.

If you hear something over
and over again, you begin to
believe it to be true.

And then, suddenly,
this is where you linger.

A Month of Sundays

People ask me all the time, "Do you miss her?
You were promised forever,
and forever ended; how did you recover?"

And this is an honest answer—

The love she had for me was an illusion.

It was not the kind of love I held for her.

It was masked in narcissism and a one-way street
designed to constantly keep me under control.

The forever I believed I had was poison.

Surviving it meant, eventually, I could find the sun
once more.

When I blew out
the candles this year,
I wished you were still
just a faceless shadow to me,
instead of a memory
that haunts every part of me.

It took strength to dig into
the parts of me I didn't want
to admit were there.

I have found that everything
starts from within—
courage to take accountability,
willingness to continue to grow,
forgiveness for the way I have been.

It'll leave you unsteady, ripped open, staggering through empty days. The guilt: for still loving them despite how difficult it got in the end. The fear: you'll never find anyone to love you ever again. The embarrassment: how did you allow someone to break you down in this way? So you split in two, one half hopeful that there is still the person you knew inside, the strength surely still existing somewhere. But then there is the other half, tired and exhausted and drained. How will they find their way back out of the hole? And you'll ask yourself, *How do I start living again?* For a while, you might find it in the bottom of a bottle or the sheets of someone else, but one day you'll understand—the winter came, and it took away the sun, and it plunged you into a darkness you never thought you'd survive. But the journey, no matter how trying, is one you take step-by-step, until you find the sun again and you bring it back home.

You don't need to be afraid
to go back and reread
your chapter.

Sometimes, the things we write
will change.

Sometimes, the sentences
we believed tied our souls together
need to be rewritten.

THE HOME THAT YOU ARE BUILDING

If I could go all the way back in time
to the day my whole life fell apart,
I'd take a deep breath before the climb
and listen to what was truly in my heart.

Sometimes, the world can be so unkind
and life knocks us right to the ground.
Some days feel impossible, for we are tired,
but beyond the hurt, this is what I have found—

A home is built from some important things,
like strength and hope and laughter too,
like the simple joy a loving memory brings
and the chance of always being able to renew.

For even when a storm brews and rages outside
and the darkness promises a long, difficult night,
for even if it is much easier to run and hide,
inside our home, we can always find the light.

When I speak, shadows
spill from my mouth.

They bind my hands,
block my vision, force
the air from my lungs.

How did I become this way,
drowning in thoughts?

Sometimes, I don't even
understand myself.

I am not sure who made you believe
that you were not a song, or a poem,
or a walk on a bright, warm day.

I cannot undo every moment that
wove together to create this idea
that you were only an afterthought,
a book at the back of the shelf,
a forgotten memory.

But I can remind you that every time
a wave crashes, and we feel like the air
is knocked out of our lungs,
there is a calmer wave that follows.

The light fades
and I am
on my own again—
holding my heart
in both hands.

I whisper
"Do not be afraid—
there is strength
in letting go."

Each and every night
I close my eyes
I leave the world
with the moon
and I am born again
when the sun rises.

It is curious the way darkness
always hands us the paintbrush,
the instrument, or the pen.

From the things that hurt us,
beautiful things are born.

It will feel as though you are the only one suffering through the darkness. As though the frustration, the anger, the bleakness only belongs to you—far too many things have gone wrong; the light at the end of the tunnel is no longer visible. But just hold on. Find the things that make you fight another day. Because something or someone will find its way to you. Full of hope, of promise, of reminders that there is still a melody in the world. The way you feel now won't be the way you feel forever.

And that was the saddest thing—
I had once believed I needed you.

I lost myself, trying so hard
to love someone else.

For months, I would run my thumb along my wedding finger, an instinctual habit. The ring was meant to symbolize forever—a promise to always keep me safe, to calm me in moments of anguish. On the day you walked out, I wondered how I was ever going to take it off. On the day the truth revealed itself, I ripped it off and threw it in a box. It took what seemed a lifetime to look at my hand the same way, not to notice the indentation of a promise that was meant to be there; not to feel anger, betrayal, fury that those promises had all been a lie. Until, one day, everything the ring meant just faded, the indentation too. It's funny, you know; once upon a time, that ring meant everything to me, and now it's just a piece of metal.

Let me tell you what is sad—the way it's never equal. It's thirty–seventy, or sixty–forty, or eighty–twenty. Someone always asks how your day was first; someone always says, "I love you," first; someone writes longer cards; someone waters, prunes, takes care of the plants, and the other person picks them. There is always someone who pulls the cart along the road, and the other person sits in it, thinking life just happens.

I will always be at home within poetry,
because it is the constant listener.

I am heard here.
I am not judged,
I am not dismissed.

There have been plenty of moments in my life
when I have been taken for granted—
but poetry always makes me feel seen.

Our minds and bodies are always connected; even when it feels as though they are on completely different pages of entirely different books, they still belong to each other. So, when your mind tells you that you are nothing, look at the sunlight glistening on your skin, listen to the beats of your heart, feel the wind on your face, smell the sweetness of the flowers in your garden, and taste the salt in the air along the shoreline. We pay so much attention to the thoughts in our mind and yet so little to the feelings on our bodies. Thoughts come and go, but when we focus on all the things we feel, we realize we are still here. You are not nothing; you are everything.

The stars will not let me sleep.
They whisper the things
I have been ignoring;
they sing of the truth
I have tried to deny.

Isn't it obvious?
We are both too afraid
to say what needs to be said.

You are you, and I am me—
but we don't fit together anymore.

For a long time, during those darker
moments in my history, I wondered if
I should leave, if I should close the
book and leave the story unfinished.

My heart was not in sync anymore,
like the night without stars, a garden
without flowers, a boat without sails.

It felt like the winter would never end.

Until, one morning, the sun filtered in
through the window and filled my room.
It washed over me in golden streams, and
as I stirred, I felt the air deep in my lungs.

In that moment, all the warm parts came
flooding back with the sunlight, like all the
ice melted away and revealed what I had
forgotten—that even in the moments the
melody and the beat are off-key, it does not
mean that the song will never be in sync again.

And I will carry this, my song, myself, forever.

Grief is all-dimensional; there are layers, pathways, crossings, and threads that intersect. It is both chaos and quiet. There are moments when something makes you laugh, and in others, nothing will. One good day, one in between, one good day, one in between; and then, there is a bad day. And it sinks you. Plummets you down into the depths of the darkness you spent the minute, hour, week climbing out of. It is the feeling of wanting to lie down in the middle of wherever you are—the supermarket, the office, the bedroom, the bathroom floor—and stay there forever. You will dream of all the ways you can undo it— the loss, the ache, the pain—and then you will rise in the morning with it all still in your heart. Such sorrow will feel loud, a storm bellowing, "Hope was here." But it is not going to ruin you, for you will also hear a whisper: "Hope still is."

The darkness can be all-consuming.

Let's not pretend that there isn't tragedy
in this world or that sometimes it feels
as though there is more bad than good.

It is a fact; bad people win, and good
people suffer, and it is not fair.

It feels easier to wrap negativity around
our shoulders like a cloak and live in it.
It is simpler to complain about things,
to let the anger blind us.

I have been there many times before,
when even rising in the morning
feels like a chore.

But I do not want to live like this—
to be so consumed by anger and negativity.

To always complain about things that don't
need to be complained about.

You lose sight of what it means to be grateful,
to be humble, to be someone who carries on.

A Month of Sundays

Those days or weeks can feel heavy;
we feel disconnected, out of touch
from the light in our lives.

The feeling can come with sudden
change or heartbreak, or it can just arrive
on our doorstep for no reason at all.

But we can accept such darkness
without allowing it to swallow us.

I know—so much easier said than done—
but I am learning to befriend such feelings,
to hold space in my heart for all.

There are woodlands in which I walk often, filled with red maple trees, and there is a particular tree, along the path I walk, that shelters me in the summer months while I read, curled up on the lowest branch. But during the winter, the darkness wraps around the woods, and the cold sets in. The trees are stripped bare. I still like to walk the woodlands, even in the winter, and I return to the same tree each day. Some days are harsher than others; some days, the fog is so dense, you can barely make out the tree at all. But on all the days, there is always something different about the tree. And I am reminded that, even during the darkest periods, new life is always emerging. The maple tree is always evolving. This is what the woods has taught me— we need the winter as much as we need the summer. The world needs the dark as much as it needs the light.

I know what it means
to be afraid of our thoughts,
especially the ones late at night.

That sinking feeling of knowing
that as soon as you lay your head
on your pillow, your mind will
begin to race and your heart ache.

But I also know there are many
magical things that dwell in
the darkness, like stars and fireflies,
like peace lilies and jellyfish—
how beautiful that is, to know that,
even in this darkness, there is more.

We have been taught to fear the winter and the harshness it brings. We have been conditioned to resist the darkness, to believe that, when such darkness comes, it consumes us. But this is not true. For even when the shadow emerges and the cloud finds its way into your mind, there is still light within your heart. It is still this light guiding us through the shadows. You do not need to suffer in silence—beautiful things can grow in the dark.

And it will hit you out of nowhere. One minute, everything feels balanced, it's a good day, and then the next, life feels far too big. It's impossible to do even the simplest things, and this makes you feel like a failure. Not just at something as simple as unloading the dishwashing but at life itself. It's easier to sleep, to hide under the covers all day and all night. To exist is to live in exhaustion. How have I stolen the joy from myself? I don't even have a reason. The darkness envelopes your soul, and the ache will eat away at you. But ache, like darkness, is shared. You are not the only person who feels these things, and when ache is shared, it feels smaller, more manageable.

It is scary to sit with these feelings
of regret, of failure, of sadness.
It is uncomfortable to lay them all
out on the table in front of you.

But this is how we make sense of them.

Our vulnerability is an important
part of us; it teaches us the way to
move forward.

UNFAITHFUL

When the truth was finally revealed,
it brought with it a long, dark night.

For every flaw you had and every flaw
I had, there I was, able to find patience.

Because I believed that you were loyal,
faithful, and committed.

I held those attributes in the highest regard;
I held *you* in the highest regard.

So, to discover that you had betrayed me,
lied to me, disrespected me, and had held
no value for me, meant that everything in
my life came tumbling down.

All the years of my life that I had spent
with you had been a waste.

You had not cared for or loved me in the
same way I had for you.

The truth was that you were incapable
of loving anyone but yourself—
and that was a gut-wrenching realization.

It broke my soul.

I have been thinking about how we are left behind—by friends, lovers, time, ourselves. One minute, someone is in our lives; the next, they are gone. One moment, we are a version of who we have always known, and the next, everything changes. It is perhaps one of the most daunting things in life, the enormity of it all, how we are just meant to carry on, to live with the grief that is left over. I suppose that is the wonder of time. One day, you are staring at a winter ground, barren and dry, and then you notice the stem of a flower regrowing, and you realize you, too, can survive the winter.

We can think of darkness
as the storm that causes chaos
or we can see such darkness as
the backdrop for the moon at night.

Grief can be everywhere, all at once—maybe it's from a sudden and unexpected loss, maybe it's drawn out over years of suffering, maybe it's because things are too heavy or the week has been one wrong turn after the other. But we have to allow people the grace to sit in their darkness, to retreat into their cave and acknowledge that dark things will always exist. For when you sit with such darkness, a curious thing happens. You begin to understand that perhaps it is not the enemy. For when you look up, along the ceiling of your cave, you'll notice it's dotted with fireflies—hope that you will come home to the light.

trust   Strength

Care

Faith

believe

hope

TAKE THE TIME

We live surrounded by the idea that we must always be doing. Everywhere you look, there is a glossy, edited picture of someone else's organized and productive life. And while the heart is always there—to inspire, to motivate, to encourage—sometimes we forget that the true message is lost, and, instead, we believe we must be succeeding, all of the time, or else it must mean we are failing. We forget that slowing down is as important as the air we breathe, that to rest is not to fail but to rejuvenate. There is a reason the woods hibernate in the winter, so come spring, they are ready for whatever may come their way.

There were so many dreams
I had when I was younger,
so many wild thoughts and
endless possibilities.

But then you get older, and
things just don't happen the
way you thought they would.

And you could be bitter about this,
disappointed, or you could take
a moment, pause, and think of all the
things that have happened that made
you smile or made tears spring to your
eyes in joy and find that gratitude.

Things have not gone the way in which you planned;
life feels as though it has shattered all around you,
no one to talk to and no one who will understand.
And in all this mess, you aren't quite sure what to do.

And despite what was taught in the very beginning—
that we are a product of our unrelenting behavior
and that if you stop or pause, you are not winning—
just know living in stillness does not make you a failure.

It is time we placed faith in learning to slow right down,
in taking a steady breath and doing the work to heal.
In listening to our hearts, every beat and every sound—
for one of the most beautiful things is choosing to feel.

I know; you were so in love with her. You wrote songs about the way you felt for her. You missed her every day. And then, someone else came along, and the pain of watching her happy with someone else was enough to make you want to sink into darkness and never return. But look at you now. All the days and months that have gone by, look what they have done, how they have helped you return, wiser and strong. I knew you would find your way back. You spent every moment thinking she was the sun and forgot you were the entire sky.

—all love

It might seem like everybody has it all figured out except you. You are getting older and still don't really know what it is you want to do—with life, a career, questions that don't ever seem to have one answer. But you don't have to have it all planned out. There are people who go their whole lives stuck in a space they committed to out of fear of what others may say because they did not take the time to listen to their own heart. So, take your time.

And I imagine all
the chapters of my life
like pressed flowers—
forever preserved.

In the colder months, the darkness settles earlier; I like to think this is because the universe knows we need more time to unravel the version of ourselves we wish to evolve from. We need to be able to think of the lessons we have learned, to mourn what we once were, so that we can welcome the person we wish to be. When we understand that change from the heart, we understand that taking the time gives us the grace to trust the process and make the start.

Courtney Peppernell

There are many things that take time,
like maturing wine and a mountain
that needs to form, like a blooming
garden and fruit from a plum tree.

All wonderful things don't just happen
without the need to grow,
much like you.

Trust that taking your time
will often lead to good things.

As for time, you will find it is the one thing that cannot be returned. Once the moment is gone, it is gone. You can always paint another picture or dream another dream; you can always find another path or watch the stars all night long. But you will never get those exact moments back. So, the more life goes on, the more time becomes the most precious thing; who you share your time with, what you dedicate your time to, how you spend your time, and what you do with your time. This is why, lately, I have been holding every moment closer, relishing in what each one means to me. How complex and yet how simple it is to be human—one moment we are here, and then we are not.

You robbed me of years of my life;
this is how I will remember you,
as a thief.

You stole those years from me,
just like you stole so many other things—
my generosity, my devotion, my heart.

You fundamentally changed
the course of my life.

I do not know how I ever found the
strength to find forgiveness for that.

But I did; not for you, but for myself.

You took years from me,
but you will not take the rest of my life.

A year ago now, I raised three little chickens—not so little anymore—who needed me in those first few days, weeks, and months of their lives. And as we navigated the time together, they saw the world for the first time, and I tried to protect them from it, only to find the moments slipping by. It wasn't until one day I realized that life was about living in every small moment as it happened. There was no need to worry about the things that I could not control, and instead it was important to be present for every little one of their victories—the first adult feather, the first time spreading their wings, the first moment of sunshine and stepping in puddles. You do not get this time back; it moves on, like most things in life, but you gain the memory forever.

If we crossed paths in another life, and you wore a different face and you did not sound like the person I had listened to for so long, I would still love you. I would love because I would know you. And I would know because I took the time to learn your soul. We leave our bodies, our memories, our moments all behind, but never our soul. It is with us from one body to the next, for every life we live. This is why when we find the other soul we come to love, we take the time to learn it.

Some days, the pressure
sitting on my shoulders
feels too much to carry.

As though with every
new step I am sinking
further into the ground.

But when I see you,
and you look at me and
remind me that the world
feels lighter when
we carry it together,
I don't feel so alone.

If time is all we have,
then I'd spend it all
with you.

There is power in slowing down,
in taking a breath between every step.

With patience comes strength.

So, while I may take my time in the walk—
I may pause to look at the sky or watch
the bees tend to the marigold—this has
given me perspective.

It has enabled me to continue walking
forward instead of backward.

That is all we can hope for—
just to keep moving forward.

When the weather began to warm, and the creatures emerged from the woods, Patience and Time sat together beside a riverbank, the sun beating down upon them.

Patience turned to Time and said, "I have brought some seedlings to plant, so that next summer we will have shade and many other things."

Carefully, Patience unraveled the little seedlings, pointing to a spot nearby: "I will plant one, and you will plant the other."

Time nodded, and together they planted the seedlings. Over the summer, they returned to the riverbank, day after day, watching the seedlings grow and tending to them. The weather only became warmer.

Time was eager to move forward, insisting one day, "We can skip all this. Let's just arrive when our trees are grown, and we will have our shade sooner."

Patience said to Time, "You must learn to slow down; we miss valuable things when we rush the process of growing."

But Time did not listen, instead choosing to rush the process of their tree growing, and in doing so Time's tree was not able to sprout many leaves or provide any shade.

Meanwhile, as the seasons passed, and the year rolled into a new one, the tree that Patience had planted grew tall, with many leaves, and soon fruit bloomed from the low-hanging branches.

At the riverbank once more, Patience invited Time to sit under their tree, in the shade, with the sweet fruit to enjoy. "If we rush to have things right now, because we want them, then we rarely get the things we truly need."

And Time agreed.

Learning what we are capable of, what we deserve, what our significance is, takes years. We don't always know who to give second chances to or who to let go of. We aren't always sure what is good for us and what isn't. But it all takes time, experience, and making mistakes. The kindest thing you can give yourself is patience—life constantly unfolds all around us, but we miss all the things hidden in the creases if we don't take our time.

Time will teach you many things: that life is a lot more
complicated than you thought at sixteen; it's more difficult,
too; it's also beautiful, all the things you've done and seen—
the way a sunrise lights up the horizon, how tea feels on
a rainy afternoon, how the stars always seem to shine for
the moon. There have been many moments when I have
struggled to come home, so afraid of all the days I may fall,
but then I am reminded of all the times I've flown.

Maybe there will always be a small part of my heart that never heals, but only because I invested everything in you. I fell for those eyes and the way you played that piano and how you would look at me as though I was the only person in the room. I thought I was going to be with you forever, the first person I really loved. But time has taught me something more valuable than healing—I don't need to forget you. I don't need that part of my heart to heal. Because you were an important lesson, and without the lesson, I wouldn't have the life I have now.

You are not too complicated, emotional, or messy. You just have standards—it is a riddle, this thing we call time, and we should not waste it on people who want to take shortcuts. Real love is taking the long way home; it's investing in the other person, layer by layer; it's spending the time because it's the simplest way to show how much you value another person. We cannot control time, but we can control how we use our time with other people.

A LETTER BACK IN TIME

The years have all stretched out before you, and you can see every moment as it passes you, like fields along the road—you should know; you have learned many things. Like how rivers never stay the same; a storm is always different, no matter how heavy the rain. Love is curious; it brings you the kind of joy where your heart feels warm and safe but also the kind of frustration where you wonder if some days are better spent alone. There is nothing more beautiful in the world, no mountain or shoreline, no city or town, than the feeling of coming home. One day, you are going to understand how important it is to take your time, to think before you leap, to go through the struggle rather than run from it. You will continue to falter every now and then—you are still human, and you are not perfect—but life has taught you to keep moving forward. It has taught you that time does not stand still for anyone, anything, or any reason—but you have carried on anyway.

And I suppose every now and then we are presented with a choice; we can either remain as we are or take the time to learn what we can be. We can choose to stay the same, or we can welcome a better version of ourselves. Some storms feel like they last an eternity, and in all the destruction, it can feel as though we will never rebuild, but once you choose to spend the time on yourself, you will find the strength within you is far stronger than you ever believed.

FIND

PERSEVERANCE

When you have been on this journey for so long, it can feel like you are repeating the same things all the time, like you are just a broken record, singing the same song, like you are the same plants that grow every spring in the flower bed or the same path taken over and over. But if you stopped and thought about what it was really like, you would realize that the world is so big: how do you know whether the words you have said aren't being heard by someone for the first time? If someone is seeing or hearing these words for the first time, and I have chosen not to repeat them, then it is the same as never saying them at all, the same as living in silence. There is always hope when we remind each other of our perseverance.

You make me feel like I can never be sad or anxious or feel the darkness swallow me whole. You make me feel like my whole existence is to make sure your feelings are always catered to. That I can't worry, that I can't feel fear, that I must always be this pillar of strength for you and everybody else around me. But I will fight to be heard; I will demand that not always being okay does not make me weak. I will take a stand for all the things that are allowed to be felt.

One day, you'll remember
that time in your life,
and it won't hurt.

It won't be filled with
the immeasurable pain
or intense suffering.

The experience of the jagged
parts of life can be unforgiving.

But you learn.

And these lessons hold your
hand in the end.

They reach for you in the
moments you believe yourself
to be drowning, to be running
on empty.

They remind you to hold on to
that strength—just keep going.

I understand what it means to be generous and fair and romantic and to feel as though these attributes are not returned to you. And you struggle with this idea of giving and not expecting anything in return versus, *Why should I give so much when I get so little back?* I know that you are exhausted, hurt, and frustrated that everything always seems to fall to you—but have hope that a day will come when you will stand tall once more; it's always the selfless who end up arriving on the bright side of the door.

Some mornings you'll wake up and the day will feel like it may take some more effort than others. You will need to remind yourself that there isn't anything wrong with you—learning to prevail and to heal wounds is not an overnight journey. You must remember love, and plant it within your soul; allow it to wrap around your body.

You cannot deny the pain
a voice
any more than you can deny
its merit and worth.

Let the pain speak.

Let it cry, yell, call out
into the wild.

This is how we prevail,
how we rise to the challenges
of the things greater than us.

A Month of Sundays

It was clear you had always
underestimated me.

You did not understand my
courage or my resolve.

In all the long years of tearing
me down, you failed to see
the fire in my heart still burning.

Here is what I admire:
my own strength.

And I am only getting stronger.

In the end, it never matters
how many tests you failed;
or when you loved someone so much,
but they didn't love you back;
or how many moments you broke
and your soul cracked and ached.

What matters are the roads on which you
forged ahead, despite all the reasons
not to.

What matters are all the things
you live for now, even if you
never meant to.

These pages have carried me through
as I wield my pen like a flame,
guiding me through the dark.

I am charging through open plains,
racing from one thought to the next.

Sometimes, I wish to scream into the
lonely night, but the moon is so beautiful,
and she makes me forget all these feelings
I am still yet to fight.

The choices you made
did not just impact me.

You were the driver,
flying down the highway,
and when you crashed,
fragments ripped through
every aspect of my life.

All those who loved me
felt the ripple of what
you had done.

They, too, had to live through
the heartache with me.

But we did live through it,
and they lent me their strength
when I needed it most—
so many people survived you.

Sometimes, it's not about saying
"it gets better" a hundred times over;
it's not about forcing curtains
open or sending notes of inspiration.

It's about reminding someone
how things aren't always easy,
and battles sometimes last forever,
but no matter the road ahead,
you'll be there together.

You're all worked up, with thoughts colliding into each other, like fallen stars exploding in space. Your hands are shaking, head splitting, heart aching as it races. The what-ifs play over and over, the need to shut it all off. All you really want is to be able to live in the moment, experience life and more without being so afraid of something as simple as walking out your door. I cannot promise that the thoughts will never be there; I cannot promise that the fear will disappear forever. But I can promise perseverance lives in your heart, and it remains with you for every step; you can walk through the world together.

On the good days,
the world felt bright,
limitless,
no journey too bold
to complete.

I wanted to bottle the feeling,
store it in my pocket
so, on the days the darkness
showed itself, I would be
ready
to bring back the bright.

If we want something badly enough, it becomes a goal. There are times when that goal will feel too great. A mountain impossible to climb, a wall keeping us out, a path too hard to find. But if we divide that goal, or split it up into many smaller goals, suddenly it becomes simpler, more achievable. Remember that skyscrapers are not built in a day; they start from the ground and gradually reach toward the sky—you must rise gradually to your dream.

You can say you have
strengths and weaknesses
or you can say you have
strengths and an opportunity
to grow.

What we do best is often limited
by the doubt we have of the things
we think we can't achieve.

But you can achieve anything
if you focus.

For all those who have gone
and become mere memories,
do not grieve for the space
they have left.

Instead, find stars to fill the void
and to shine light over the darkness.

Let this light create new memories,
new feelings, new adventures.

As you move through life,
fill every empty hole with forgiveness,
new moments to embrace, and remind
yourself you are not your mistakes.

At any moment when the world forgets your worth, I hope you remember that your voice matters. That you have every right to say no; that it is your body, your mind, your soul. I hope you find strength to carry on, to find energy when people wear you down. Never underestimate the fire that lies within; it is a flame that burns bright and is needed in the times when you feel you cannot win.

People associate shadows with darkness—
where monsters dwell and horrible
things happen.

But on a hot summer day, shadows
from the trees keep us cool; on a wall,
with a light, shadows can tell a story;
in a parking lot when you are alone,
your shadow reminds you that you're not.

All things are not lost;
even light comes from the shadows.

There is a moment when a baby bird must leave the nest for the first time, and surely it wonders whether the leap is too great; if it cannot fly, then it will fall. Life is like this. Sometimes we are too afraid to take the risk, too afraid we will fall before we can fly. But in these moments, close your eyes, take a deep breath, and remember there is so much that exists beyond the nest. If you never take the leap, you will never know what you are capable of.

On this journey, you will lose many things. Someone you love; friends you thought would always be there; favorite clothes, toys, and books; time and memories. But the person you will be is worth the loss, worth the struggle, worth the fight. You are the star of your story; you are the warrior, the captain, the light.

Eventually, I overcame you. It was the most difficult chapter of my life, the most painful path, the hardest journey. I was forced to untangle the threads that were woven between our souls, something I never thought I would need to do. I had truly believed they would never fray, split, or break, and I was wrong. To accept this took strength I never thought I had. To confront every memory, sift through the fragments of the life we had shared, and reclaim my sense of self required a profound shift in all that I believed I knew. Your significance faded, but the lessons I learned remained. And in this newfound purpose of overcoming, I found my freedom.

A lotus flower grows underwater,
in dark and muddy depths, often
struggling each day to rise toward
the sunlight—
but it persists and rises anyway.

We must endure to reach the light.

A STORY OF PERSEVERANCE

Once, there was a young girl who loved to write. She would write all day, every day, pages and pages. As the girl grew, she began to invest longer hours in her craft. She soon joined a writing class, during which the teacher instructed the completion of a final paper. After working on the paper for weeks, the girl handed it in. But the teacher said to her, "This is not the correct way to write. It is not how this genre is traditionally styled. You must go back and rewrite this." The girl went home and considered the teacher's remarks. She decided she wanted to use her own voice and share this with the world. So, she returned to the class and told the teacher this. But the teacher insisted that she must write the way that was taught, and if she chose not to, then she would never reach her goals or dreams. The teacher said that a high mark could not be awarded if she did not rewrite the paper. The girl thought long and hard about what the teacher had said. Perhaps the teacher was right, and she should just follow the rules, but in the end, she decided that she could not change who she was or the way she wanted to write, so she told the teacher she would not be changing her story.

And so, the teacher gave her an F.

Now, years later, the same girl has millions of books sold in bookstores all around the world and continues to live her dream, using her own voice, every single day.

When someone tells you that you cannot do something, do not allow them to steal your dreams. Your persistence and your determination will carry your soul, and your courage will remind you to follow your heart.

The ant maps out a path and follows it. If it is moved off the path, it will return; if an obstacle is put in its way, it will find a way around to get back to the path. No matter the challenge, the ant will always try again—you, too, must encourage your willingness to stay on course.

The woodpecker strikes its beak on the tree, knowing that each single strike will produce minimal change but that, in the end, by staying consistent, the accumulation of each strike will lead to the ultimate goal of breaking down the wood, and so the woodpecker continues. You, too, must not ignore your small wins; your persistence to get there is a success in itself.

The bee devotes its entire existence to making honey for other bees in the hive. Together, they work tirelessly so that no bee in the hive goes without. It is important to have yourself, but it is equally important to embrace the help of others.

There will come
a defining moment,
perhaps not today
or tomorrow or the
next, but someday
you will realize
what you are worth,
and you will be steadfast
in not accepting anything less.

—I hope this for you

Some days, it feels like I am just screaming to a brick wall, that I am dragging my feet along a pathway that only ever leads to a dead end, that I am climbing stairs that go nowhere. Where do you go when you have reached the limit of your limits? What do you do when you cannot keep repeating the same days, when your own feelings feel foreign to you? How can it be that the walls are caving in all around you, that the house is collapsing in on itself, and nobody notices?

A Month of Sundays

So many things in life
will often disappoint you,
and you'll have to swim through
agony over moments not going
the way you thought they would.

But all good things require perseverance.

It is a difficult truth—people will make you feel like you are just the old flashlight that sits at the back of the drawer, only ever used in a storm. That you are just an old sweater hanging in the far side of the closet, out of reach. That you are the old pair of shoes discarded under the stairs, collecting dust. Or the old favorite toy, replaced with something new. It will be up to you to put aside the flurry of hurtful feelings this brings and demand the respect you deserve; such perseverance, such grit and determination to stand up for yourself, well, it will ask for everything you embody—your breath, your light, your patience, your whole entire self. You might not see it today, but when you arrive at your becoming, and you stand a little taller in front of that mirror, you will understand it all had value.

VALUE
THE CLARITY

You have this moment of clarity, and it could be about anything—your job, your relationship, a friend, your family, the person you are, or the way you walk through the world—you have this breakthrough moment, and you decide that you just don't want life to be this way anymore. You no longer want to be treated unfairly, shouldering and tolerating what you shouldn't have to. You want more for yourself, because you know you deserve more. You want people to listen to you, to acknowledge that you are deserving of great things, to appreciate all the things you do, to show you gratitude for the way you care for the people around you.

And I am telling you, once you have this moment of clarity, it's like shedding a layer of yourself, and you can suddenly see the person you are underneath. They have been fighting this whole time to reach the surface, and now they are here.

Set them free.

Once upon a time, they made you feel special. As though you were the first person to hear all their secrets, know their heart, know all there was to know about them. They promised they would never leave, that they would continue sharing the deepest parts of themselves with you, only to rip that away from you, making you feel a little less deserving, a little less worthy. Perhaps the lesson is that you will never be the first to hear the secrets of someone else; you will never be the first to keep them or to lose them. But you will be someone's last, and that is worth holding on to. It takes strength to understand this, to convince your heart to beat on the same page as your mind.

When you broke my heart, I had forgotten who I was. I was lost—a ship with no port, in a current dragging me further and further into the universe—deeply afraid to love someone new, for what would they think of me, someone who no longer cared to feel joy or warmth? What would they do with all the darkness? And, perhaps, even more frightening of a thought, what would I think of a love that wasn't you? But through moonlight, and mornings spent searching the sky for clues, I realized I never needed you, or your love, or the ache it brought. I was more than the current and more than crashing waves. I was the whole ocean, and the universe knew my name; it was welcoming me home.

You are never the same
version of yourself.

You are changing with
every breath.

Which is why the unknown
is so frightening and growing
can be so uncomfortable.

But you just continue.

Every new version is better
than the version before.

Every new version is equally
needed by your soul.

How can you say you have empathy
or that you understand when you
treat anxiety as a burden, something
that ruins your plans?

How can you say that you know what
anxiety feels like, and yet if someone
else is drowning, you act like they are
the problem, just someone hollow?

How can you say that you have battled
such things face-to-face, when your
actions show me you will never know
what it means to be someone who often
feels overwhelmed or out of place?

It's your lack of responsibility
and accountability that unraveled
the image I had of you.

The way you would claim that the
things that needed doing were second
to the things that you wanted to do.

It is simple to say that rafters are
equally as important as the beam;
both contribute to the house.

But if the beam decides it will no
longer accept the behavior of the
rafters—the house collapses.

THE TRUTH TELLER

I lived through hell for so many months, always suspecting but never uncovering. And when I was discarded, there were hundreds of little things I kept turning over. I was made to feel as though it was all in my head. But it wasn't. Because the truth always finds a way. It found me, because someone had enough backbone to finally tell me the truth.

To this person, I say, I know you feel guilt, for having to keep the secret for so long. But it was never your burden to bear. You were told you would be ruining four lives, and yet it was the choices of two that had brought all the walls crashing down.

You gave me clarity, and my gratitude to you will live in my heart until the end of time.

The truth wears many faces,
diverse and wide.

It hides in pockets and corners,
where secrets reside.

Through clarity, we find our freedom,
a weight lifted high.
For nothing ever good comes from
deceit and webs of lies.

When secrets are revealed, it disperses
darkness, a light illuminating the way;
it leads us closer to peace
with each passing day.

I uncovered you for who you really were. The mask you had so carefully worn all these years cracked many times, but, one day, it completely fell apart. I finally saw you, and all the things I had been made to believe faded away—you were cruel to me; you had no patience, no empathy. The reconstruction of all that I knew was messy. It was not rebuilt in a day. Every minute took miles of hard work. But I built something in the end, a stronger version of me, and it was unbreakable.

Hell hath no fury,
they say, as though
a woman is not entitled
to feel anger toward a person
who has hurt her deeply.

A Month of Sundays

You threw your entire life away with me.

The fact you had everything handed to you
on a silver platter, how good I was to you,
the stars in my eyes every time I looked at you.

And it was all for someone as equally toxic
as you.

You discarded me for someone unwilling to
even meet you halfway.

—laughing face emoji

There are so many things you have done for the last time: driven past an old building now torn down, had a cup of coffee with someone you loved who is no longer here, learned to ride a bike for the very first time, danced at an event that was a once-in-a-lifetime. So many little things, and we don't even realize. This is what makes your ability to cherish every moment so important—it could be the last.

The stars never intended
for your heart and love
to be taken for granted.

You are not obligated
to waste your time on
people or in spaces
where it is not wanted,
appreciated, or tended to.

Instead, invest your time
in the things that ultimately
give you joy, fulfillment,
and a sense of purpose.

When you lose something, it's very easy to focus on this loss without seeing anything else. So, you spiral, and suddenly the only things you can think about are the things you do not have or the opportunities that have been taken away from you. People will tell you to breathe, that the feeling won't last forever, and to focus on yourself—and these are all true in their own ways—but you also must remember that we will not always see life clearly or understand things with a sense of certainty. We will always have confusion, ambiguity, and insecurity, and these things will often weave chaos along our path, but we must still walk the path anyway. In those moments, ask yourself what you haven't lost, list the things you still have, and try to find reason in your fear, because this is what it is: it is fear of having to start again without the thing you lost. And let me tell you something: you can start again.

Someone asked me recently if I ever just take the win. And I suppose it made me think of all the times I have shrunk myself into the corner, of the way I avoid the spotlight, the way I consider myself a background character rather than the lead. I know that it is difficult to stand tall in spaces that are filled with people who are loud, people who demand the attention, people who speak over you—it makes you feel invisible—but I suppose you just have to stare down the loudest person in the room and say, "You will not silence me." I am not going to sit in the corner, or in the shadows, or on the sidelines anymore. I am not going to be made to feel unseeable, that my feelings do not matter, that I am too sensitive, or that I take things too personally. It is no laughing matter when someone makes you feel as though your voice doesn't matter, that you cannot speak, that you are unloved, a burden, or an inconvenience. Stand up to these people. They do not get to diminish your worth.

There once were two builders, and they were each building a home. The first builder rose early, like each morning, and went to the store. He gathered the strongest materials, arrived at the job site, and began work on the home. The second builder, however, had been restless the night before and therefore slept in. He arrived at the store later than anticipated, and most of the strongest materials were gone, so he quickly chose alternatives. He, too, headed to his job site and began to build, even though he knew these materials were not the best.

Over time, the houses were built, and the foundations of each house were very different. One day, there was a big storm. The wind howled, lightning struck, and the rain pelted the two houses. The first house stood against the storm and withstood any damage. It had been built with a strong foundation, but the second house was weaker, and it crumbled.

We must be honest—with ourselves and with others. Honest with how we carry ourselves, our thoughts and feelings, and our intentions. When we speak honestly, and we take accountability for our actions, it becomes easier to communicate with others. The foundations we have with others are built on trust, and trust is what helps us withstand the harshness of life.

It would be easier if the lessons life taught us were simpler—if they were not difficult or hurtful or dark. If, when we were born, we had a clear path mapped out in front of us and we knew exactly what we wanted to do, who we wanted to love, and what we wanted to spend our time doing. But if this were life, then it would be no life at all. What I have learned, more than patience, more than light versus darkness, more than setting boundaries and having open conversations, is practice. Because life takes practice, and it will always take practice. You must practice managing periods of darkness as equally as periods of light; you must practice patience and kindness and navigating the lessons that life throws at you. You must practice setting boundaries and having honest conversations; the clarity that you will attain by doing this will, for the most part, find you in unexpected ways.

We live in a world that can often feel disrupted, dark, and overwhelming, and in such a world, your mind must remain sharp—a chef does not cook with a blunt knife. This is the same for approaching the world with our minds busy, distracted, and out of focus. You need to slice through difficult truths and commit to a lifetime of ever evolving.

The waters flow, a mirror reflecting the sky—each ripple a reminder of the beauty under the surface. For every breath you take, allow yourself to sink deeper into the water's depths, feel every doubt, every worry, every frustration leave your body as you absorb the stillness around you and let the hurt go. There is peace here that eludes us elsewhere, a calmness that enables us to see the world in a new way. When you emerge from such waters, you will be renewed, and while you will always carry the memory, it will no longer be in your way.

The answers I had been desperately
searching for just appeared one day,
as though the fog had cleared,
the veil had lifted,
the curtains pulled open.

I could finally see.

In the stillness of my thoughts and
of my heart, the doubt became
a distant memory.

I could make sense of the noise
all around me.

I could see the way I was being treated.

I knew that I needed to change course,
to stand up and say, "This is not okay."

I needed to remind myself of what I
was worth, of what I deserved, of the
things I believed in.

So, I did—I chose myself.

And I have not and will not look back.

One day, in the later parts of winter, I drove for hours along the highlands. I stopped in a small town and climbed a tower with two hundred and forty-six steps. When I reached the top, up high, the air was thin, and I was above the clouds. The world seemed so small below, cars just small dots along the road, houses like little building blocks, and the surrounding mountains engulfed me. It was here where the things that bothered me faded away; I could see the world with new eyes, free from the noise and fray. It was here where I was able to shed the burdens that held me down and reach a place of peace, where perspective could be found.

We are always rushing, and often,
in the commotion of our lives,
we lose sight of the things that are
important, and our minds narrow,
trapping us in the present.

But with patience, and an open mind,
we can learn to view things differently.

If we look back on each day, each year,
we can understand the mistakes we've
made and learn from the paths we've
chosen in the past—with each step we take,
we gain perspective; we are always
moving closer to our purpose.

A Month of Sundays

When the shadow of doubt and confusion
obscures the path we are meant to take,
we search for signs of faith and resolution—
a way to ease our minds and heartache.

Know that, with time, you'll find the way;
the fog will lift and so too your despair.
And all the worries that lead you astray
will fade like mist in the morning air.

A new day dawns and with it a new song
to fill your heart with promise once more—
to remind you that here is where you really
belong, that you are braver than you were before.

In a little town on the outskirts of the city once lived a young girl fascinated by the stars. She would spend many nights gazing up at the sky, enthralled by the magic of the distant points of light twinkling in the darkness. She dreamed of exploring the universe, discovering new stars, and uncovering the secrets of the sky. But as time went on and the young girl grew older, her passion faded. The pressures of life caught up with her—studying, work, responsibilities, and obligations—and they demanded all her time and energy, leaving no space in her heart for stargazing.

One evening, while sitting on her balcony, exhausted from the day, the woman noticed a bright star in the sky. It shone brighter than the others, its light beckoning to her through the sky. For the first time in many years, the woman felt the spark of the little girl she had once been.

As the weeks went on, she found herself drawn back to the sky. Every chance she would get, she would stay up late into the night, watching the stars and imagining all the possibilities they held. She began to remember the magic she had felt as a young girl. She realized then that while the path to following her true dreams may be precarious, difficult, and full of setbacks, she knew it was worth it for the feeling of being fulfilled.

So, the woman set course for a new path in her life, intrigued by where the stars would take her.

ACCEPT THE GROWTH

A Month of Sundays

You will never go back
to the person you once were.

Time will pass, and the months
will start and end without
a hello or a goodbye.

The courage to accept such change
doesn't always come easily.
There will be days when you hold on to
old habits in the same way you cling
to the memories you wish to keep forever.

But the things that no longer serve us
do not have a place in our tomorrow—
to grow is not a threat but a gift.

Truthfully, I am still learning to allow people to make their own mistakes—and it's never easy. When you care for someone, you want the best for them. If you know something could hurt them, you want to protect them from it. But, sometimes, the people you love need to sit with the consequences of their own decisions. You cannot fix people, any more than you can breathe air for them. You must understand that by always taking the difficulty out of their lesson, you are preventing them from ever learning.

It is always about effort.
Even if the said effort is
little by little, step-by-step,
moment by moment.

You will feel small some days,
and on others you will feel as
though you are the whole universe.

Even on the days you feel small,
carry on with the same effort.

It is through consistency you
will find the space to grow,
and, little by little,
you will find the place to heal.

We hold on
because we are
afraid of change.

They say everything
happens in time—
even though we often
wish to skip ahead
and already arrive.

But stagnant waters
never truly flow,
for it is in the rapids
we learn and grow.

In my dreams,
we didn't grow apart;
instead, we lived the
lifetime we promised
each other.

All the days and nights pass by,
the dawn rises and the dusk sets,
and I feel myself ever evolving,
becoming stronger and more adept.

I reach for the sky, like a sunflower
seeking the light, knowing my roots
are an anchor, the courage to fight.

With every passing year, I shed a
new layer, leaving behind the person
I've been, becoming someone newer,
bolder, a force the world hasn't seen.

The road before me will always be long
and more often than not unforgiving,
but I know I can handle whatever
challenges life may be bringing.

With open arms, I embrace every trial
and lesson—I can face them all.
For, with every leap I take, I am growing
steadily and standing tall.

But it wasn't just you who had hurt me. It was the other person. You both made choices; you both deliberately chose to act. The anger I felt for her was insurmountable. I imagined all the ways I could get back at her, to seek revenge, to destroy her life in the way she had destroyed mine. But, in the end, I had to step back and look at her for what she really was—she was nothing. I had tried to assign value to her; I had tried to like her, to think of her as someone worthy of my time and of my energy. But others would often say they felt uneasy, uncomfortable, unsure in her presence. I held the anger for her, I made space for it, and then I let it go.

There was no choice; I had to go through every single process, and, like all things in existence, time moved ceaselessly forward. It became a delicate dance of progression. I had been called along this ever-changing path to undergo the biggest transformation of my life. It began in chaos and shock and later dimmed to a subtle whisper, a voice always murmuring in the dark, stirring me to acknowledge that change was inevitable. In this unfolding for all the things I once knew, I was stripped, layer by layer, until all that was left was the core of my true self. I was vulnerable, exposed in every way, but I had also been liberated from all the things that had been holding me back.

There will be times the journey
feels like a fire raging within,
burning through everything we love,
this fiery blaze that tests our resolve.

Uncertainty crushes you, a weight
sitting firmly on your chest,
forcing the air right out of your lungs.

But the more you persevere, the more
you notice the subtle shifts.

Our perspective broadens, and with it
comes a deeper understanding
of the things we truly seek.

Change unfolds in the same way
a delicate blossom unfurls its petals.
It demands our patience and our
resilience to the elements
we cannot control.

The growing will always take time;
it's the kind of process that weaves
threads, merging the old with the new.

It allows us to release what no longer
serves us.

And then we are given the chance to
redefine the things that bring us joy.

And suddenly, one day, you will be standing in your kitchen, and you'll wonder where all the years went. Did time really move by so quickly—every birthday, anniversary, vacation, or holiday season? Did you catalog every memory so that, by the end of the journey, they'd pass by in your mind like scenes in a movie? I hope you pause, every now and then, to reflect on how every season changes; to know that through struggle we learn to adapt, to thrive, and to be; that in all the years of growing, we eventually become free.

It is not a simple thing, to accept how often life changes. That the world changes, your friends change, the person you love will change, that you, yourself, will change. Everything changes, always, constantly, forever. Just like the sky fills with clouds and the rain falls and then the water returns to the sky. The way life changes is a story as old as time—and with said change come realizations, like the need to believe in yourself more, your right to say no, that you don't have to be everywhere at once, that it is not your responsibility to please all those around you. It is your life, and you get to decide how the change guides you.

They always said your twenties were the building blocks—you figure it all out, and you carefully craft your life. But this is not what I have lived. I am still building, each and every day, still learning and shaping. And there are many things I still do not understand, like the way a person can say a million wonderful things about you, but it's the one critique you hold on to for months; or that pit in your stomach when someone leaves you on "read," and you blame yourself rather than the simplest answer: perhaps they are just busy in their day. Like why the best part of the day, when the sky is golden and full of color, only lasts an hour; or why, when your heart is broken, time feels like it goes by second by second, but when you are happy, the years fly by in the blink of an eye. But there is something, a truth that has sprouted in this garden: we are not in control; the train will leave the station at the time the train leaves, with or without us—and I suppose there is something beautiful in this.

Deep in the darkness, I needed to remind
myself that I was not an option or second
choice to be made. I was not an afterthought
to be set aside and sparingly displayed.

I was a person, with a heart and soul, who
didn't deserve to be left in broken parts
instead of loved as a whole.

I was not someone's backup plan, a last resort,
or just a safety net. I was not just a convenience
to be used when wanted and then suddenly retired.

And I say this from the depths of all that I am—
I am a person to be seen, not to be tossed away
and treated terribly; I am worthy of being loved,
and I deserve to be a priority.

This is a truth about me—I am afraid of flying. There is no point in denying it or running from it; a fact is a fact. But, as it happens, I am also afraid of change. At the airport one day, I had a plane to catch, and, like many airports, it was busy, people moving to and from departure and arrival gates, long lines, and a little chaos. Funny how life also mirrors this. My heart begged me to go home, for there is security in things staying the same, everything needing a place, days having structure and order. The idea of flying through the sky, surrendering to the clouds, so far from the ground, had always been terrifying, and this day wasn't any different. The fear had rooted me to the ground, where life was surely certain and safe. But my soul insisted I board that plane, and when I did, it reminded me that change was frightening and unpredictable at first, but it is also the link between new places and new experiences. Every flight I caught thereafter reminded me to see the world in a different way, that the sky was not the limit to what I could achieve. And now, each time I board a plane, I am reminded that the things that frighten us are often the things that lead us to the best journeys.

It's a lifelong journey, isn't it—
being able to put yourself and
your needs first.

For some people, the idea of saying no,
of choosing yourself, of meeting your
own priorities can be uncomfortable.

There may be a person whom you did
everything for, and they still weren't happy.
For whom you put their needs above your own,
and this is never the way things should be.

If that person thinks that the grass is greener
on the other side, then let them go over
the hills, and focus on rebuilding your garden.

Sometimes, failure is the only option—we don't talk enough about this. When you chase a dream, you will almost always need support. There are many people in this world who are not awarded the same fortune as others, who are not dealt the cards they need in order to prop the house up. There are bills to pay, families to support, food and shelter to provide. Some people don't have the opportunities to leave everything behind, to take risks, to take a leap. It is okay to put dreams on hold, or to have them realized and achieved in other ways. Failure is sometimes the only option, but that does not mean you are the failure.

It was crippling, to think of life being alone. In this loneliness was all the heartache entwined with every memory surrounding me. I had never felt grief like this. I had never felt the weight of such darkness. Never in my life had I thought I would feel such pain, such a gut-wrenching, pull-apart, sinking pit of despair. It hurt; it hurt like nothing I had ever experienced. How could this happen to me? How could the person I loved more than anything break me in this way? After I had given everything—my heart, my soul, my entire being. But, despite such loneliness, such crippling sadness, I also knew that my life was not meant to be lived this way, in agony. I needed to remind myself that, somewhere in this world, there was someone who would love me the way I deserved.

I suppose I can see the difference
in who I was last year compared
with who I am now.

I speak more.

For the things I want and the things
that bother me.

You can't expect to go your whole
life allowing other people to take
advantage of you—

you are worth more than this.

There is strength found
in the things we say
and how we choose to
navigate our way—

When we lend a shoulder
for someone to lean upon,
we are reminded of all the
light we are born from.

There is a small truth in caring
about someone else's fears,
and all the things they hold dear,
for in that act of kindness shown,
we, ourselves, are forever grown.

The most difficult part of growing
is knowing that you will leave some
people behind, but the beauty that
comes from such loss is found in
the space for new people to arrive.

Courtney Peppernell

I have been doing this for so long now,
pouring every piece of myself into pages,
sometimes I wonder if anyone is still listening.

It is me in between every line, it is my soul
in between every word, it is my heart in
between every chapter.

But I have days when I feel so alone—
and I know that I am not, I know;
it's just this feeling, so overwhelming,
I don't know which way is up or down.

Here is a lesson I have learned about respect: There were two gardens, and in each were clusters of plotted plants. In the first garden, the plants were not taken care of; it was messy and unkept. When people would visit this garden, they would often leave garbage, and they would walk all over the flower beds. In the second garden, the plants were very well taken care of. They bloomed and radiated. People did not leave garbage, and they did not walk over the flower beds. If the garden is unwatered, unpruned, or left to rot, then this is how someone else will see the garden as well. You must respect yourself first and demand that others do the same.

Time changed you, and, in most ways,
it changed us.

I still want to believe that in some time
and place we can be happy again.

But, for now, it feels as though this month
of Sundays will never end.

The suffering is immeasurable.

The thought that you no longer love me,
are no longer happy with me, with this life
that I so desperately tried to give you.

And now, it is painted on every wall of this
house, that I must choose to go on without
you, to grow separately from you, even if
it was the last thing I wanted to do.

I took the time to grow. I sat with my thoughts, my feelings, my grief—day in and day out, I sat with such things, and I told myself that, in order to heal, I had to go through it. I was not going to run from it, I was not going to pretend the change hadn't arrived, and I was not going to mask the sadness. I stepped each step, I climbed each rung on the ladder, I moved forward. And then, one day, the sun rose, and I felt alive, happy, grateful for the change that had happened. People heal in their own ways, they move forward at their own pace, they find the things that stitch them back together again, and they thrive in the newness. Sit with the things that make you feel as though the world is ending; sit with them, acknowledge them, let them go, and open yourself to the things that will keep you putting one foot in front of the other.

I arrived at a place where I knew I did not need another to complete me, that I was beautiful and strong and able to move mountains on my own—and when this settled in my heart, and the years I had spent feeling unloved, underappreciated, and small became just a distant memory, I met her. And even though I knew I could still move mountains on my own, she was the kind of person you take with you, and you watch the sky for hours and know that even if the sky is painted in one hundred beautiful colors, they still don't compare to her.

After the dust had settled, and I could look to the horizon again and see the sun, I was faced with an impossible fork in the road. If I ventured down one path, my heart would remain closed. How could I possibly trust another again, after I had been treated so poorly? This thing called love, it would not do. I'd opened my doors to the worst kind of person—I would not open them again.

Or if I took the other path, I could accept that while I could not change the time I had wasted, or the signs I had ignored, I could change how much it impacted my life thereafter. And in doing so, open myself up to someone who was worthy.

I chose the second path, and I walked very slowly in the beginning. I took note of the wildflowers, blooming through the seasons; I was hesitant to run or climb or jump. But eventually I met someone along the way—she loves sunflowers and kookaburras; she has a laugh that warms a day, eyes that light up a night, and is always the kindest person in the room.

It is possible to love once more, so long as you don't lock the door.

We will always be changing.
It is a lifelong process.

It never truly ends.

It does not matter how many
times you circle the sun; there
will be more lessons to learn.

So, embrace them as you continue
to walk the path, open your arms
to different experiences, be willing
to rewrite chapters, accept that you
will always be growing.

LET LOVE IN

It wasn't a fleeting thing,
the day my self-worth walked
out the door.

It left without a word, or a second
glance, and it did not return for days,
weeks, months.

Believe me when I say, to write of love
or of hope became so foreign to me.
Suddenly, it felt as though I no longer
knew the words.

When I thought of myself, I thought of
such dreadful things. There was nowhere
I could go that did not feel like a deep,
dark place, this hole inside my heart,
unforgiving and unsafe. Was I still a home?
Was I still living and breathing? This didn't
feel real, didn't feel like life. For the longest
time, love could never exist again.

But then, thinking of all the little things,
a hand to hold, flowers on a doorstep,
a deep breath when the days felt
insurmountable, perhaps I could give
all those things to myself.

My whole life was a love letter to you, and one day you stopped reading. I was not sure why. I had given every letter, every word, every sentence, and, at the end of the page, you tossed it away like it meant nothing. When you are on the road, if a branch falls, and you cannot go around, you remove the branch. This is the same for your life and removing the things that are not good for you. But there will never be a day when there is not something worth doing—kindness to be spread, a smile to give, an outstretched hand for someone who needs to take it. So, perhaps, I can write letters for others, and if those letters bring joy, then that will be enough.

You looked at me, as I sat,
staring out at the skyline,
sadness in my eyes, and you said,
"I know it feels like the world is ending,
but imagine one day, when the hurt
has subsided and every move you make
doesn't feel like you are moving the
stars and more, you find someone
who doesn't expect you to carry
everything, who stands beside you
and says, 'I see all the baggage,
but you are not alone in shouldering
all the weight.'"

Courtney Peppernell

I like to think that
you aren't gone forever,
at least not the version
of you I loved.

I like to think that
you are somewhere in the
universe, heart still beating,
even if it is not beating in
sync with mine.

It gives me hope, you see,
to think that in another life,
it would have worked.

Of course, when you have loved for so long, and the love ends, you mourn this. Then comes the day when you venture out into the world again, and it is terrifying to think of meeting someone new. Of opening yourself up again, of being vulnerable, of wearing your heart on your sleeve. The idea that you have to go through those initial steps, someone asking what your favorite color is, what movies you like to watch, what your story is—and it seems so mediocre and false—when you have gone to the depths before, how could you find yourself back to the surface once more? But you have forgotten, all things start from somewhere, especially the good things. If a flower wilts, it must seek to grow again, which means the seed must sprout from the soil.

We are all different,
this much is evidently true,
but something most of us want
is just to matter.

To know that, on someone's hand,
we are counted as important.

For even if love isn't the answer
to every little thing, without it,
we forget the joy that life can bring.

I have lost which way is north;
I am somewhere in the woods,
and I cannot find my way out.

It's frightening, this darkness—
where did all the light go?

But perhaps this is the point:
I don't need to go north;
I can go east or west or south too.

I understand, this colossal sadness—when it feels like the joy has been stripped from every ounce of your being. It feels as though there is only murk and mud, and you are doing everything you can to wade through.

One day, I remember standing at the edge, the ocean waves rolling around where I stood. A light appeared, and it asked me, "Who has hurt you so badly?" and I replied, "The person I loved most."

"And what now?" this light asked.

"I do not know, for now I don't think I will ever love again."

We stood at that edge, for what seemed like forever and a day, until the light finally said, "But you felt this love so deeply that, when you lost it, life ached in a way that seemed like eternity. But here you are, still feeling."

"What does it all mean?"

"That, one day, when the dust has settled and the pain subsides, you will return to love, and it will wrap you tightly in its arms and be what you deserve."

A Month of Sundays

I have loved you
with my whole heart,

but I have forgotten
the love I deserve too.

And even if I miss you
in all the things I do—

I just miss myself too.

It's much easier said than done, to shelve the worry, to not think of your life as cascading by so quickly you barely have time to check if your shoelaces are tied. But in all the worry, and the sleepless nights, you may miss a simple truth— that, somewhere out there, there is something or someone waiting for you. And that something or someone will bring you immense joy. You will be happy, you will be loved, you will be cherished. And not for all the things you think but for the simple things: the warmth of your smile, the light in your eyes, the kindness that spreads from your soul to the air around you. So, if you consume yourself in the dread, and in the misery, you will miss that feeling of opening the door and letting something beautiful happen to you.

We had a home, and we loved that home—more than anything—but the home had not been built soundly. It was not as simple as some chipped paint that could be easily fixed with a fresh coat; there were cracks in the foundation. And over time, those cracks had grown, until one day, the home collapsed. In order to rebuild the home, we had to cross a bridge. And under the bridge were murky waters filled with bitterness and resentment. The water needed to be drained. Don't you see? Happy homes are hard work. Love is not enough—you need trust, communication, honesty, loyalty, and some laughter along the way.

It was March when the storm ripped through my sleepy little town. I'd carefully built every structure, planted flowers in garden beds, trees in the parkways, hung lights on every windowsill. I'd poured all my love into it all, and, in one storm, it was all torn apart. Carnage lay on every doorstep, destruction on every road, heartache everywhere I looked. I was broken all of April, all of May through October, half of November, three quarters through December— because when things end, it hurts. I knew I must accept such endings, for March eventually returned, and so, too, will love, in new beginnings.

To exist in this world is not always easy—some days, the darkness seeps from every corner and spreads so far, it takes all the color along with it. But this is why the love you hold in your soul will always make the world softer. Every hug when you hold on a little longer, mountains dusted in snow, a favorite song shared with a stranger, a book that made you feel alive. Yes, in the absence of someone you loved, the world can feel nothing but a shadow, but there are many things that make this life bearable. So you hold on to those things and begin to move again, one small step, a day at a time, and you drink in every bit of love the world leaves behind.

The betrayal lingers;
it creeps its way into
every facet of your being
and takes up residence.

It becomes part of you—
the way you hold yourself,
your ability to think and feel.

The foundations of your faith
crumble beneath you, so you are
left trying to stand on shaky ground.
There is a semblance of relief for
feeling like you are no longer whole.

You sleep with a hollow heart;
you wake with a broken soul.

But, during such times, you begin
to relearn your inner compass;
you embrace your intuition once more,
to understand forgiveness as an ally,
even on the days you are sobbing
on your living room floor.

You find a resurgence in unexpected
places—a smile from a stranger,
a ladybug on your windowsill,
bursts of joy that leave you fulfilled.

There are better days waiting for you
when trust in love blooms anew.

The birds were always there,
even on the days when it felt
the sun didn't rise—

they were always there.

They waited for me
to greet them on the balcony,
and it took awhile
(oh, did it take some time).

I missed days, weeks, years,
but I arrived,

and the birds were waiting.

I was the world, and, suddenly, every tectonic plate shifted, and I was changed catastrophically. I knew others could see it, for it's always written on someone, when their heart has suffered. Mine had shrunk so small, I was unsure if it would ever grow again. I looked inside, wondering where it went; all that was there was a giant gaping hole. But, over time, I was reminded that my heart was still there, beyond the suffering. I knew it would grow again; it would open its doors and let those worthy pass through.

And, now, I wake up in the morning and I still have coffee, but I can hear the trees, how they whisper sweet nothings, and I see the sky for all its wonder, and I smell the flowers I've been growing—there is honeysuckle sprawled across the fence line. I care, I really do, about the dreams of others; I like to remind people of their worth. The chickens are somewhere in the yard, the dogs, too; there is music playing, I wave to the neighbors, and I am thankful I chose to go on. It took me the longest time to arrive, but I did, and I am so glad I did.

You are worthy of someone
who encourages you to follow
your dreams.

Someone who understands life
has lessons and we all learn them
at different times and in different
ways.

You are worthy of someone who
can't wait to see you, who insists
on a hug a little longer than the last.

Someone who treasures you in
the present, who looks forward
to the future and loves you in
spite of your past.

There you were, and I didn't want
to close my eyes and wonder
what might have been.

I didn't want life to pass me by,
not knowing how your hand
felt in mine.

So, if you don't mind, I'd like to
spell out the way I feel for you—
I am turning, crashing and burning
every time you say hello.

I am floating, dreaming, falling
every time I see your face.

There are all these moments I want
with you, because my favorite part
of every day is when I finally see you.

The first moment when I met you,
I swear my heart skipped a beat.
It may sound a little silly,
but I knew I was finally complete.

You are poetry to me,
even after all this time,
and, my love, let me tell you,
you are the light of my life.

Home is wherever you may be;
you bring me joy every day.
All the little things you do,
your smile takes my breath away.

Even after all this time.
And, my love, let me tell you,
you are the light of my life.

Life may twist and, surely, it will bend
as we go along this road,
but on me, darling, you can depend.

You are poetry to me,
even after all this time,
and, my love, let me tell you,
you are the light of my life.

It's a curious thing, the way
someone collides with your world
and they change every second,
every day, and every moment
of your life.

Suddenly, there is this person
you've never known before,
and now you can't imagine
your world without them.

If you don't feel loved right now, I hope you find it here—have you been drinking enough water, did you stop to look at the sky today, are you laughing even if you don't feel like it? Are you putting on your sneakers and going for a walk, maybe sitting by the lake, ordering an ice cream cone late at night? Are you looking in the mirror, breathing in, telling yourself you are beautiful even if you don't feel it? Are you texting people back even if you don't feel like talking? Are you still getting tickets to your favorite shows? Are you staying away from the things that make you feel hollow? It's a bad day, or a bad week, or maybe a bad year, but you still deserve to be here. I see you, and my heart explodes like confetti, and it fills empty skies.

Tomorrow is not promised; this I know to be true. I feel it deep down inside, to the very root of my core. It is not easy to look at things and feel love when you feel so empty. But perhaps such devastation can wait. We don't have to look at the world as though it is ending. We can sit here, underneath this pear tree, and we can watch the sky, the planes slicing through the clouds. We can laugh, wonder what the forest would look like if the leaves were always red. I keep thinking I have grown so old, I don't remember what it feels like to be young. So, today, I will feel that childish wonder, remember the purity of a Popsicle in the middle of summer, the joy in a snow day, the feeling of rolling down a hill. For so many Septembers, life felt dull and gray, but, today, the color has returned.

—let's sit awhile

I filled my days with gifs of sunflowers and videos of small animals, anything to remind me there was still joy in the world. I felt so alone, so out of love, so unwanted and damaged. But then I googled old houses, and it led me to the map where images from the past stay glued to the screen. And there was a cottage with ivy growing along the walls and roses in the front garden. There was a Ford Thunderbird in the driveway and a cat sitting on the front porch. I wondered if I walked inside what there would be. Maybe pancakes served on the kitchen counter, the French doors open to the courtyard, a gentle breeze filtering through. I thought I'd like to stay in this house forever; maybe the love would seep from the wooden floors and climb its way around my grieving heart. And then I saw two people wrapped in an embrace by the front door, maybe saying hello or maybe saying goodbye; it didn't matter—because love would always be the past, the present, and the future. It didn't matter the path the river took if the current changed or the bank dried up, for the rains would come and the water would always return.

You will not have everything; it is not possible. But you can have a snack at midnight or a walk in the rain. You can have the moonlight reflected in your eyes and count the stars until you sleep. You can have that comfortable old couch and the favorite sweater you never got rid of. You can have the lemon tree in the backyard and the dog lying at the foot of your bed. And you can be certain of someone and something, and you deserve to have that calmness and to be loved with the same certainty.

We are the notes in the most
beautiful song I have ever known—
always rising and falling,
a melody that makes us fly,
a soundtrack that brings us home.

I know that, when I am with you,
I feel every beat in my heart,
a rhythm that carries us
through every new start.

There is never a day
your voice is not music to my ears,
your eyes the stars across a stage,
your whole being lyrics on a page.

In every moment, and all the love
we share together,
know that you are the song
I could listen to forever.

This is what I now know to be true—that the person I was writing about all these long years, I had not yet met. She existed deep in the very pockets of my heart, and I had been searching for her, lying to myself every day that I had already found her, because I had not. But, then, one day, when I least expected our paths to cross, they did, and I met her by the ocean. She arrived with the sun in her hair and a smile that made me forget what I was going to say. And when she talked of the things that made the world shine, I felt a pull I had not felt in a long time. Now, every time I think of the sun, of the ocean, of all that is good in this world, I think of her.

You deserve to be kissed
every minute of every day,
to be reminded of how beautiful
you are—that when you smile,
it pours from your heart and it
lights up the entire sky.

You deserve to be cared for,
to be kept safe, to have honest
conversations with someone who
could listen to you for hours.

Believe me when I say
I see your whole soul.

She told me she loves sunflowers,
and so I wanted to plant a field
of them for her.

She told me she loves tea,
so I wanted to always make her a cup
in the late afternoon.

She told me she loves to read,
so I wanted to write for her every
morning and every night.

She told me I was beautiful and she
saw me for who I was,
so I wanted to remind her she is
every star in the night sky, burning bright.

Maybe it's in the way you look at me or the smile you have every time I walk through the door, or maybe it's in the way we can talk for hours and your hand fits in mine, but there is a beat in my heart that makes me want to keep you safe, for you to know that I care, that I want every good thing for you—that, when I am with you, I feel like I am finally home.

I want you to be surrounded by love. To find comfort in so many things—like the warmth around a campfire or the tranquility of waves along the shore, like sunsets and hikes and the first day of spring. The familiar scent of fresh-baked brownies streaming through an open window, the soft hand of someone you love, your favorite song you play all day. It's in these moments, when we feel connected to something bigger than ourselves, all the anguish fades away and we see clearly there is always a chance to begin again. This is how you will always let love in.

PRACTICE SELF-COMPASSION

It was not a profound discovery, rather a thought, small at first, until it grew, the way ivy slowly spreads over forgotten buildings. And I thought of a younger me, so filled with hope and willing to walk every step with her head held high. *How, after all these years, had she convinced herself it was better to hide? How could we have let this happen?* And it all played the way old movies do, with vignette and grain. The way she did not wear short sleeves, for she did not like her arms. She styled her hair the same each day, afraid that any change would not shape her face in the right way. She always did her makeup, to try to hide her face, and never wore clothes that would define her shape. Her body had become an enemy rather than the ship that sailed her around the world. Every time she looked at her reflection, there was no compassion in her eyes. So, I reminded her that while all the lost years could not return, it did not mean that we could not take back the rest of our life. To her, I say, there is light in the dimples of your smile, stories in the freckles across your nose, and there is promise in all that you are, as sure as this life flows.

Too many times you have apologized
for the thoughts inside your mind.
Are they too deep, dark, or chaotic?
Are they thoughts anyone else would
have the heart to listen to?

But you don't need to apologize any
more than you need a reason to explain.

Because, despite all the thoughts, you
deserve to be loved all the same.

You will look at your own reflection
and not like what you see,
picking at the folds of your skin,
wanting to change your hair,
not knowing what the next step is
or where to begin.

You will feel lonely, notice the empty
space beside you in bed, wish terrible
things on the people who have hurt you,
unstitched you, thread by thread.

But there will be relief to all the ache.
You will travel roads you never thought
you'd stumble upon; your feet will hold
you steady, and the night won't feel so long.

So, when you look in the mirror again,
you'll see the reflection is beautiful instead.

All the hours you have spent
running from yourself,
comparing yourself to others,
forcing yourself to please everyone,
are all hours wasted.

You are not worthless for setting
boundaries; you are not weak for
making yourself number one.

The things you love are the spine
for which your body holds a soul;
there is no need to neglect
taking care of you.

A Month of Sundays

It's true; I struggle with myself sometimes,
finding it hard to be my own friend.

I often wonder if I will find the place I belong—
maybe in the arms of someone I can call home.

Will I find the sun once more and dance in
fields of green; will laughter return to me,
like the rain to the stream?

Will these memories rise from ash into light;
will I become the person I've always thought
I could be—will I ever be enough for just me?

There will be many words
you punish yourself with:

"I am not good enough,
I am a failure,
I am the problem."

You will rehearse them so often,
they will feel like weeds planted
in your mind, suffocating and angry.

But weeds can be tended to.

Start with the words:

"I am beautiful,
I am worthy,
I am enough."

—watch as you begin to regrow

It felt like an entire lifetime,
the years you lived buried
and hidden in the shadows.

Someone always telling you
what to wear, how to speak,
what not to do.

Yes, it was a lifetime,
a dark chapter.

One that you can now shed—

You no longer need to live to
please others. You are here,
for you, a soul worthy to flourish
in all the joyful things that bring
you peace.

Rather than sit in a broken home, with memories scattered everywhere, I stood; I fled. And while I know you can never outrun the things you are meant to feel, I do know that, sometimes, being somewhere new can give you the perspective you have lost sight of.

So, there I was, sleeping in a barn, under skies filled with stars, a fire burning outside, fireflies glowing along the tree line, and as I stared into the flames, I had a vision that my soul was sitting beside me.

All that I was, am, and will be.

So, I looked at my soul, and I said, "I am so sorry for the things that have hurt you, the people who have damaged you beyond what you believed could be repaired. You are more than what you think you are. You are wonderful and kind and beautiful, and you go through the world with strength and resilience, and you hold your head high.

"There are many stages of this grief that you feel; it is a lengthy process, a journey you did not envision to be on, but you will fight your way through it. Let all this blame you have placed upon your shoulders burn in these flames; lay them to rest. You are not this brokenness, and you will rise from these ashes."

—this one is for you

At night, I would stare at our picture on the wall—my favorite one, the sun glowing behind us, eyes locked, hands entwined. It would fill me with sorrow, with anger and despair, trying to make sense of it all. Had this been some fabricated story, a detailed list of lies? The time could be three in the morning or two in the afternoon; time didn't matter, for I would begin to cry—*Why did you have to absolutely ruin everything?*—an empty heart, my entire existence now rendered fragile. You brought me down to my knees, begging the stars to answer, for how could they allow something like this to happen to me? There were moments I wished we'd never met, heart torn apart with misery, full of regret. But, then, one night, I took the picture down, and I replaced it with something that made me smile—

and I slept.

The air is humid, and the sky grows darker,
clouds gathering on the horizon, blotting
out the sun.

The wind accelerates, and when the storm
arrives, it shakes the trees so violently, I think
they will come crashing down.

But they don't; they are still there in the morning.

The storm hits me every night when I am alone.
But still, I am here the next day.

Once, I happened upon a small goldfinch, fallen from its tree—bright yellow against the tall grass in which it lay injured. I took the bird home, and I spent time nursing it back to health. When its strength was restored, it was time to release it back to the sky, and yet there was a part of me that did not want to let the bird go. Surely it was safer with me, away from the cruel world in which it could be harmed. The world was a risk. There were many things that could go wrong; it could be injured again or worse. And, after a moment, I realized that the bird was me. For so long, I had retreated, hidden myself away, but in doing so, I was also missing out on all the good the wild could give me—a chance to fly, to spread my wings, to be free. I was holding myself back, torturing myself, and I knew that such suffering was not what I deserved. I could not do that to this little bird, and I could not do that to myself. So I did let the bird go, and as I watched it soar high into the skies above, I promised myself I would do the same.

I had cared for this person for so long,
what was I going to do with all this love I had?

I'd filled my days with caring—I'd managed the home,
I'd worked so hard to achieve a comfortable lifestyle,
I'd paid the bills, I'd cooked dinners, I'd done the laundry,
I'd taken care of nearly everything, and I'd lent my ear,
my shoulder, my heart to whatever they needed.

And, then, one day, they threw it all back in my face.

So, I pleaded with Compassion, "What am I supposed to
do? There is no one to care for now; where do I store it all?"

And Compassion said to me, "Have you ever thought,
in your wildest dreams, and in all the caring that you do,
that perhaps that person could be you?"

There I was, and I was truly at the bottom of a well. It was dark, cold, bitter, and I felt so alone. The thing is, I could see the light above; I knew it was there, and I knew I would be able to climb up one day. I would fight my way back into the warmth and the light of the day. But I also needed to be in the well. I needed to hit that rock bottom, to live in it, to feel it, to find all the pieces that had been shattered around me and pull them back into my soul. There are many times in life when we will be at the bottom of a dark and lonely well, but we must spend our time there, for it is in that well we remind ourselves we have the capability of climbing back out.

The value you see in yourself is not always visible, nor is it easy to cultivate. It is much like being in a room filled with boxes, each one demanding to be opened. And, in every box, there are different challenges that will be released— negative thoughts about yourself, fear of the unknown, limiting beliefs, or comparison with others. These are difficult boxes to open. But they must be opened all the same. For when you open these boxes and you sit with all these thoughts and feelings, you understand that you are so much more than them. The value comes from recognizing your strengths. The negative thoughts are not the truth of your soul, the unknown is not to be feared but to be embraced, you are only limited by yourself, others will not be you and you will not be them, you were not created that way. So, if you have forgotten, let me remind you—you hold so much value.

In all the time I had to think things through, I came to understand that I belonged with someone who chose to stay, who understood and recognized the life that had been built. It was a life filled with devotion, love, support, and understanding, and it was still not enough for you. I realized that I belonged with someone who wanted to work on themselves to be better, to be a partner, to be someone who thought of me and of us and not only of themselves. And through the journey, you filled yourself with people, but I filled myself with the world. The spiral of a mesquite tree, the color of wildflowers, the sounds of warblers, the trickle of a waterfall as it flowed to the river. I have always known what is important in this life, and I don't deserve someone who doesn't appreciate the magic of my heart—all my love needed to be poured into something that would carry it proudly and safely and treasure how beautiful it is.

I know what it is like to have been cheated on, lied to, trust completely severed. The person I loved more than life was unfaithful and then kept that lie to themselves for more than a year, with no shame, no guilt, no remorse. But it is always when the heart breaks that the mind awakens. Though this betrayal brought immense suffering, a deep ache that ran through my heart, my veins, and my bones, it also reminded me that none of it was my fault. People make choices every minute of every day, and people have to live with these choices. If you, too, have been betrayed by someone you loved more than anything, know this: it was not your fault, you were not to blame, you deserved better.

You had tunnel vision; you no longer truly saw me. I am not sure you ever really did. I gave you everything, my entire heart, soul, and being—and it still wasn't enough. You blamed me, and I sat in this blame, wondering what I could have done more. If only I had been more adventurous, more confident, more exceptional. But then I realized that I *was* all of these things. It was you who had kept me small. You who had tried to tie me to the corner and refused to let me fly. There was nothing more I could have done; it was all a reflection on you, the person you truly are. The illusion came crashing down around you when I honored my truth. I was too good for you.

I refused to cry. I told myself that, if I cried, it would make the pain real. But the truth is, she had detonated a bomb inside me, and I was filled with shrapnel and carnage. The only way to release such infliction is to just let it all go. So, I began to set aside time every day just to cry, let the pain seep free from my heart and out into the air around me. For the longest time, the windows had been closed, and, one day, I opened them, tears streaming down my face. But the pain floated through, out into the open, and even if it took many days, it subsided.

We are human, and imperfection is woven into our fabric. People make mistakes. But some mistakes bring a certain grief that feels as though it rots away your soul. I understand, I truly do, the idea that if you hold no animosity in your heart, it will make life more bearable. And, yes, in more ways than one, it does—but you are allowed to hold space for anger. You can do the work and move past the wrongs that were done to you. You can find strength to realize the betrayals are reflections of others and not yourself. But if you wish to block them out, if you never want to speak to them ever again, you can do that too. You don't need to justify how you cope. You can scream into an open space about all the time you wasted believing someone wouldn't dare hurt you in such a way. You can feel disgust for them, and for yourself, for not seeing all the pointed signs. But the funny thing about compassion is that it ultimately begins with having it for yourself. You are not perfect, and the suffering will feel as though it will last for eternity, but if it's any consolation—it doesn't.

It felt like I had been robbed, that I just wasted 7 years, 5 months; 2,739 days; 65,736 hours. I would never get that time back, and the path that lay in front of me was filled with unknowns. I was so angry, so hurt at all the time that had been taken from me and all the moments I was going to have to spend healing from the damage you had caused. Until, one day, staring out at the sun rising over the hill, I decided I would not give you any more hours, days, months, or years. It was my time now. I don't know why some people cannot see worth, value, a good heart—I do not know why they are always seeking something more—but I do know that the path I am to take will be filled with reminding myself, *You are free now; there is nothing you cannot do.*

Our stories are very different; you were right about this. But while you seem to think life should only be about fun, parties, a good time, I know what life really is. You need to be able to find the joy in the mundane, the beauty in hardship, the necessity of struggle. I don't deserve someone who ignores all the responsibilities of life, who wants someone else to take care of them for her. I did deserve someone who would go to the grocery store with me looking for ice cream and believe that life was beautiful in just that. The biggest mistake I made was believing that person was you.

Compassion for myself is what pulled me through the storm; it was the very thing that lifted the rubble I had been buried under for so long. It took time, as I had been led falsely down a path for many years; I had married her, I had given her my life. But then the illusion self-destructed, and all that I thought I knew, and all that I thought she was, was not the truth. I had been tricked. It was not false, my feelings, this deep love that I had cultivated, but hers was. I had to sit with such compassion, to be kind to myself, to remind myself I would be filled with shame and blame myself for not seeing clearly when so many people tried to warn me. For ignoring her behavior, for choosing not to face the kind of person she really was. But I am okay; I am better than I was before. She is no longer holding me back.

HOPE FOR TOMORROW

It was as though my whole world had become a haunted house. And in the house were ghosts of all the things I did not want to feel. How could I allow myself to feel it all— the anger, the heartache, the rage of betrayal, the never-ending sadness, the confusion. I wanted to become numb; I wanted the thoughts to just end. So, I shut every single door, unwilling to open them, too afraid of the horror that lay behind. Until I realized that, despite locking every door, the ghosts were still there. They were still on the other side. The energy seeping into the walls, hiding in the rafters, consuming the garden outside and withering the flowers. I knew I needed to open the doors, and when I did, what happened was not what I had expected. The ghosts wrapped themselves around me, told me all those things needed to be felt but that they would also pass. Things were going to be well; the past would not always hurt so much.

Hope leaves us and returns as though nothing in between happened. As though we were not sprawled across the floor, sobbing our heart out in its absence. It arrives and fills our soul with joy, confidence, an aura of "I can do anything," and then it leaves, and we are tossed back into the darkness, searching for the light again. And, if I could guess, I would think it does this on purpose. "Listen carefully," Hope says. "Your ability to wade yourself through such despair will always bring me back again. You are hope," it says softly, "and hope is you."

Maybe hope is just
in the way you feel it.

How the break of a new day
fills you with strength,
how every goal you meet
renews your beliefs.

How every step you take
reminds you of what you
can achieve.

Hope exists because you feel it,
so let hope wash over you.

Lyrebirds are known for
their remarkable ability
to mimic various sounds
from the environment.

Every day, I hear lyrebirds
in the forest behind my house.

They sound like lasers, slicing
through the ground cover and
forest floor.

I listened to those trills
every day for months.
And, over time, I began to think
of them as promises—

If I could hear those sounds
every day, it meant I was still
here, still breathing, still listening.

There is a story I want you to picture—it is set in my backyard. To start, I will paint this picture for you. I live on top of a rolling hill; at my fence line are woods. The trees hang over the railing; plants and flowers are sprawled everywhere you look. There are vines that wrap themselves around an old greenhouse; there are logs scattered in different places. Near the old greenhouse, I have built a chicken coop; there are hanging pots of herbs and marigold, and lavender grows along the retaining wall above. I sit here in the mornings as the sunlight rises from the east. It was peaceful, at least until I discovered I had unwanted visitors. In the night, a rat would visit, searching for leftover morsels from the chicken feed. As you can imagine, this could not continue. Every person I knew told me to kill the rat. They are vermin, they are rodents, they need to be eradicated. Yes, the little thief did need to leave, but I did not want to harm it. Instead, I bought some cages, and I set them up in the hopes it would find its way inside and I could rehome it. This took weeks. They seem to be a lot smarter than anyone gives them credit for. Even so, I persisted. Eventually, it trusted the cage enough to crawl inside, and I was able to catch this little thief and remove it from my property. I decided to release it somewhere new, into farmlands and tall grass, somewhere open and free. I thought of other people in the same situation who would have likely killed the rat, who would have never given it the chance. But I also thought of others, like me, who wouldn't have harmed it either. They are out here in this world, and they are patient with us. They wait to gain our trust, and, even when they hold it, they choose not to harm us.

I think of this each morning I sit in the coop and watch the sunrise—hope rising with it.

I never believed I could hurt so much, that there would be nothing left inside of me. I am no stranger to the ache of life; I have felt it many times through the years. But the ache I felt when the person I loved most broke my trust, undid everything I knew about her, and discarded me like I was nothing more than trash was an ache I do not wish on anyone. It's the sort of storm that brings trees down, when you feel you must live on low-hanging branches for knowing at some point you would be shaken out of the tree and when you fell at least it wouldn't be from up high. But this is the beautiful thing about life after storms: it goes on, and it's worth living for.

In the midst of my entire world falling apart—the trauma, the anger, the desperate need for understanding—my friend sat me down. He said, "I know you are hurting; I know that your heart feels as though it is somewhere else, very far away, in a place only reserved for those who have been broken beyond repair, but you are not these things." He said, "You have carried burdens for so long, you have forgotten what it means to be truly cared for; this person was not good to you, they were selfish, they took from you, they never gave." He said, "Every time you think of her, I want you to think of a day when you meet someone who chooses to be your equal, who wants to carry the load of life with you instead of watching you struggle to climb every hill. If you had remained trapped with her, then you would never have the opportunity to meet someone like this. You are free," he said. "You are free now."

I had every intention
of being alone for the
longest time, doors closed,
soul locked, heart left in
an abandoned building.

Nothing would divert
these untrusting eyes.

And then I saw you.

Imagine this—

You attend family events by yourself, and there's no longer a feeling of failure or guilt that you need to bring someone along. You are happy because your life has meaning simply by being with yourself. And, then, one day, you meet an equal, someone who wants to take as much responsibility and accountability for your lives together. There is no hope of this if you settle for things less than you deserve.

That was the worst thing you did—aside from the selfishness, the unfaithfulness, the betrayal—it was the false hope that shattered me. You imploded my life, then you came back, and you made me believe you would do anything. You tricked me into thinking you were holding yourself accountable, that you loved me enough to look inward, that losing me wasn't an option. Only to ruin me all over again. You were spineless, weak, a coward. I don't know if there is a single word in all the languages in the world to describe what you did, but it was a cruel thing to do to someone who had only ever been kind to you.

The silver lining in all of it was that I was able to look inward—I could never treat someone the way you treated me, and I know that holds meaning.

The darkness offers you
a place to tend to your soul—
as you wait for brighter
days to come.

And they will come.

Courtney Peppernell

Your face changes
every time I remember you;
so does your laugh—
it alters,
you change shape,
until, all at once,
you are not the same,
and neither am I.

Instead, there is someone else,
someone with a genuine presence,
a true, beautiful soul—
she's out there somewhere,
waiting, hoping, believing in us.

In the depths of the grief, I built little buildings. I would sit for hours at my dining table crafting them—I built a magic emporium, a bakery, an art studio, and a library. My whole life had come crashing down, everything was upside down, there seemed to be nothing in reach, and nothing I could hold on to. But those buildings were something I could control. I could choose to block everything else out and only focus on painting windows, building furniture, twisting and weaving little plants. And, then, in the end, I would complete each one, and I would look at them and feel like not all things needed to be broken, that there was hope things could be rebuilt.

Courtney Peppernell

And I suppose that is what gave me the most hope—
that the people in my life knew of my character;
the people in yours also knew.

But when it came to you, people didn't have
the best things to say.

You were described as arrogant and pretentious,
as someone others could not understand how I ever loved.

The world could see the truth, even if it took me a thousand
moments to truly see.

But I see now.

That was the greatest struggle, how could I write
of hope when I had none? This terrible thing had
happened to me, and I could no longer see the light
or joy. So, did it make me a fraud, to write of such things
when I truly believed they were no longer real?

Many people asked me, "Do you ever go back and read
the things you have penned before?"
The answer was always no—once they were penned,
they were only memories, some so painful, to read
them again would be to remember the pain.

But then, one evening, I did go back, and, instead, I found
what I had never expected to find—myself.

It was, after all, me who had written of hope, of finding
love after carnage, of discovering strength after
years of fear.

As though, in all the many words, I had really been talking
to myself. I had been writing of the love I had wanted,
but it had not been given to me. I had been writing of the
courage I had buried deep down inside.

I am still here within all these words.

Courtney Peppernell

I had built a thousand dreams around you—
I had lived my life, always thinking of you,
of us.

Every step I took was always with you in mind.
And then you ruined the dream. As though you
took me apart, piece by piece, and the wind
carried them off somewhere.

My greatest fear became the idea that I would
be changed, that I would not think of love
or look at people the same.

Instead, I would turn cold; the anger would
consume me, rot me from the inside out.

Yet, I learned. It took time, but I learned to
hold space. I learned to walk again, to laugh
once more, to see the good.

I did change; you had forever changed me.

But it was I who stopped you from taking
all the parts of me you never appreciated.

In those initial weeks, after the shock had subsided, I disappeared. I packed the car, and I drove down the coastline, and I found myself in a house by the ocean, high up on the cliffs, with a wraparound balcony. I spent hours on that balcony, staring at the waves, how they changed with the tides. They would crash against the rocks, sea spray and foam soaring into the air, and then they would calm, and the waters were still. Boats drifted along the horizon, the sky changed colors in the dawn and dusk, sheep grazed on the hill. Life would always be here, I concluded, even if it felt it had been drained from me. The days would still return, even if I felt empty on many. The sun would continue rising—there would always be hope for tomorrow.

But look at you,
my dear friend said,
at how strong you became
even in spite of them.

So now that they are gone,
imagine all that you can become.

The fall whispered change through the trees, like a warning to me; life as I knew it was coming to an end. Even though I found beauty in the gold, crimson, and amber, and the softening of the sun, I knew things were altering, and it was a realization that felt impossible to face. Like so many things, I could not outrun the inevitable, and winter that year took hold in such a way I never thought I would survive. The air every morning was frigid, frost leaving delicate messages on my windowsills. The trees were still, darkened, quiet. I was lost, heartbroken, wondering if the warmth would ever return. But springtime breathed new life in the slumbering earth. The world awakened, and I, too, felt the revival. And summer brought an ease to my soul; the sky stretched endlessly, adorned with billowing clouds. The laughter that filled sun-drenched days restored something in me that I thought had long been buried—that I could love life again. Time was an eternal cycle, a never-ending dance, and, even if in the depths of the cold I thought it was not possible for me to move forward, I learned to dance again.

That was the beautiful thing
about my garden, I could always
taste the pollen.

The trees weren't going anywhere;
the birds would always return.

The rosemary and the mint
continued growing.

When darkened skies
gather near, and you are
filled with doubt and
consumed with fear—
steady your soul, and keep
an open heart, for hope
finds ways to grace each part.

Through every challenge,
a lesson lies, a chance for
growth to surely fly—
and all the stories yet to be told
are silver linings waiting to unfold.

My mama said to me,
as tears streamed down my face—
"No matter this heartache, or the
path now staring you in the face,
you will find happiness again and
find joy once more;
there is nothing in this world
that could ever change your core.

"And while you have been broken,
left with ache, burden, and torment,
you must remember that she was
never worth your discontent.

"She has stolen minutes, days, and years;
she has desecrated your trust and
brought forward all your fears—
so, give her nothing more."

And, so, I decided—

In my heart, my mind, my soul,
you don't belong here anymore.

We hope for protection,
healing, and comfort.

We hope for guidance,
for love, for family.

We hope for wisdom,
for a voice of reason,
a reminder that all will
be well.

And, on the sleepless nights,
may the stars lead you
back home,
to believe in every soul,
across every galaxy.

When I learned of the infidelity, the very foundation of what I thought I knew exploded. My heart had once bloomed with promises of loyalty, trust, and honesty. But a shadow had crept in, shrouding everything in deceit's cruel cloak. I had dismissed so many things, ignored them, turned away, but the truth always finds a way. In the aftermath, fury, disbelief, the kind of sadness that crushes you. And the doubt permeated every memory. It destroyed once-cherished moments. It ripped apart the love I had for her. It decimated my sense of self-worth. Trust became an elusive spectator, haunting all my future connections. It cast a long, dark shadow over the idea of ever opening myself up to love again. I was constantly reminded of the pain and suffering I had endured. Yet, amid the wreckage was a small yet powerful reminder—I am not defined by the actions of another. The path home was arduous—the memory of such betrayal lingered—but it was no longer in my way. My soul would one day embrace a love that was faithful.

That moment as the sun
begins to descend,
when you exhale a deep breath
and realize you made it one more day.

That is the moment you have come home,
the moment you have stayed for,
the moment you have won.

I am thinking about the ones
who have endured the long
darkness of the night.

When the moon and stars are
nowhere to be found,
the thoughts are loud, and the
heart is heavy and restless.

My hope is that when the sun
rises, so, too, will their strength,
so, too, their will to carry on.

Many people would tell me, "Beautiful soul, you dodged a bullet in her." But the truth is, I did not dodge a bullet. The bullet hit me, and it landed. But it went right through, a clean shot. It did not explode and desecrate vital organs. Yes, it hurt; yes, it took me so much time to heal; yes, it would always be something that happened to me. But it was not fatal. I was still alive, I was still here, I still had my whole life to live.

You must remember your spirit. It lives within you. Even when buried by darkness and despair, it still beats in every step you take. In the times we have retreated far into the cave and it seems there is no way forward, look for hope in the embrace of a loved one, in the hues of a sunrise, the sway of trees, the magic of music, and acts of kindness. Your spirit lives in the power of dreams and the belief for better days ahead. The stories of unimaginable heartache and hardship are stories of surviving; they encourage faith that you, too, can face every challenge. There is strength in your vulnerability and your persistence to learn from every struggle. In life, hope finds its deepest roots in the unwavering belief that, despite difficult circumstances, there is always a reason to keep going; there is always a thread of possibility, a lighthouse guiding us toward moments that have yet to be written.

A Month of Sundays

A month of Sundays can feel like
the longest and darkest winter
of your life, when doubt and ache
find reprieve and dreams feel lost
and forgotten, like whispers on the eve.

The weight of heavy burdens and betrayal
leave you feeling confused and alone,
and, in these stolen moments, you'll wonder
how you will ever make it back home.

It is a truth that the mountain crumbles
down around you and spreads shadows far
and wide, but it is also a truth that you
have the strength to rise again and to survive.

For in the stillness of your cave, time takes
pause so we may savor every breath and
listen to life's true cause.

In the chapters of time, despite every challenge
and every fear, the light eventually returns
and with it your voice emerging into a new day—
"I am still here."

YOUR PROMISES

During your own month of Sundays, write down promises to yourself.

_____

_____

_____

_____

_____

_____

_____

_____

_____

_____

_____

_____

_____

_____

_____

_____

_____

_____

_____

_____

_____

_____

_____

_____

_____

_____

_____

_____

_____

_____

_____

_____

_____

_____

_____

_____

_____

_____

_____

_____

_____

_____

_____

_____

_____

_____

_____

_____

_____

_____

_____

_____

_____

_____

_____

_____

_____

_____

_____

_____

_____

_____

_____

_____

_____

_____

_____

_____

_____

_____

_____

_____

_____

_____

_____

_____

_____

_____

_____

_____

_____

_____

_____

_____

_____

_____

_____

_____

_____

_____

_____

_____

_____

Thank you for reading this book.

I hope you enjoyed reading it as much as I enjoyed writing
it. You can stay up to date with all my latest news and
projects via my website, www.peppernell.com.

Feel free to write to me via courtney@pepperbooks.org.

Pillow Thoughts app now available on iOS and Android
stores, worldwide and on all devices—download yours
today for your daily poetry!

Andrews McMeel Publishing
a division of Andrews McMeel Universal
1130 Walnut Street, Kansas City, Missouri 64106

www.andrewsmcmeel.com

24 25 26 27 28 TEN 10 9 8 7 6 5 4 3 2 1

ISBN: 978-1-5248-8674-5

Library of Congress Control Number: 2024930396

Editor: Patty Rice
Art Director: Diane Marsh
Production Editor: Elizabeth A. Garcia
Production Manager: Shona Burns